THE LITTLE BOOK OF
GIRL POWER

The Wit and Wisdom
of The Spice Girls

THE LITTLE BOOK OF
GIRL POWER

The Wit and Wisdom
of The Spice Girls

First published in Great Britain in 2019 by Trapeze
an imprint of The Orion Publishing Group Ltd
Carmelite House, 50 Victoria Embankment
London EC4Y 0DZ

An Hachette UK Company

1 3 5 7 9 10 8 6 4 2

A CIP catalogue record for this book is
available from the British Library.

ISBN Hardback 978 1 40919 160 5

Printed in Italy

www.orionbooks.co.uk

CONTENTS

'PRINCESS DIANA . . . SHE HAD
REAL GIRL POWER.'

GERI HALLIWELL
MTV Awards, 1997

'WE'RE ABOUT EQUALITY AND BRINGING
EVERYONE TOGETHER.'

EMMA BUNTON

Lorraine, 12 November 2018

'WE GIRLS HAVE

GOT BALLS.'

GERI HALLIWELL
American radio interview, 1997

'WE'RE NOT SAYING TO GIRLS TO BE A PARTICULAR WAY, WE'RE JUST SAYING "BE YOURSELF".'

THE BIG BREAKFAST INTERVIEW
6 March 1997

'THE SPICE GIRLS DO SEEM TO LIVE ON AND ON.
MAYBE THAT'S BECAUSE WE HAD A POLITICAL
MESSAGE THAT STILL REVERBERATES.
GIRL POWER. STRONG WOMEN.'

VICTORIA BECKHAM
Marie Claire, 6 October 2010

'THE FUTURE IS

FEMALE!'

SPICE GIRLS: GIRL POWER!
1997

'THE MESSAGE WE'RE PUTTING ACROSS IS,
"WE'RE DOING IT, GIRLS, SO CAN YOU. EVEN
IF YOU HAVE TO SHOUT A BIT LOUDER, BARGE
THROUGH ALL THESE PEOPLE, THEN DO IT."'

EMMA BUNTON

Big Issue, December 1996

'EXCUSE ME! THIS IS ABOUT GIRL POWER;
THIS ISN'T ABOUT PICKING UP GUYS . . . WE
DON'T NEED MEN TO CONTROL OUR LIVES.
WE CONTROL OUR LIVES ANYWAY.'

MELANIE BROWN
American radio interview, 1997

'GIRL POWER IS ABOUT

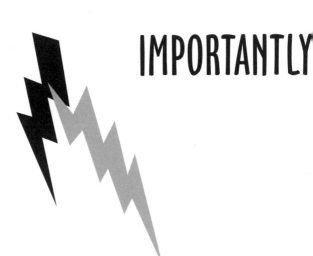

IMPORTANTLY'

HAVING FUN AND MOST

ACCEPTING

WHO YOU ARE.'

VICTORIA BECKHAM
Giving You Everything, 2007

'WE WERE JUST FIVE GIRLS WHO WEREN'T ALL THAT GREAT INDIVIDUALLY, BUT TOGETHER, WE WERE PRETTY GREAT! THAT'S REAL "GIRL POWER": BE WHO YOU ARE, DO WHAT YOU LIKE AND BE FRIENDS WITH OTHER GIRLS!'

VICTORIA BECKHAM

Q&A with Fern Mallis, New York City, 3 June 2015

'I THINK THERE'S A CLASSIC SPEECH THAT NELSON MANDELA DID AND I CAN'T REMEMBER EXACTLY BUT YOU MENTIONED ABOUT NEVER SUPPRESS YOURSELF, NEVER MAKE YOURSELF FEEL SMALL FOR OTHERS' INSECURITIES AND THAT'S WHAT GIRL POWER'S ALL ABOUT SO I THINK WE'RE ON THE SAME LEVEL, IN THAT VIEW.'

GERI HALLIWELL

when she met Nelson Mandela in 1997

'WE PUT

GIRL POWER

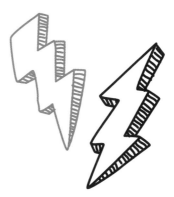

IN THE DICTIONARY.'

MELANIE BROWN
Today Tonight interview, December 1998

'IT WAS ALL ABOUT BOYS, BOYS, BOYS, BOYS. BOYS SELL RECORDS, BOYS SELL VIDEOS, BOYS SELL MAGAZINES AND WE WERE LIKE, NO, COME ON, IT'S TIME TO CHANGE, IT'S ABOUT GIRLS. THIS IS GIRL POWER.'

VICTORIA BECKHAM
Giving You Everything, 2007

'GIRL POWER IS ABOUT BEING INDIVIDUAL.'

EMMA BUNTON

MUCH, 1997

'WHEN I CAME OUT OF

I SCREAMED

MY MOTHER'S WOMB,

"GIRL POWER!"'

GERI HALLIWELL

Egos and Icons, 4 April 1999

'WE'RE JUST VERY SPICY.'

VICTORIA BECKHAM

Spice Girls — Wild! in Concert, 17 January 1998

'THERE IS A NEW ATTITUDE, GIRLS ARE TAKING CONTROL. IF YOU WANT TO WEAR A SHORT SKIRT, THEN YOU GO ON AND WEAR IT. YOU SHOULD WEAR WHAT YOU WANT.'

MELANIE CHISHOLM

Big Issue, December 1996

FAME

'WE ARE FAR TOO IMPERFECT TO WORK IN A MANUFACTURED BAND AND IT DIDN'T WORK, SO WE WENT AWAY AND WROTE OUR OWN STUFF, MANAGED OURSELVES AND CREATED THE SPICE GIRLS' GIRL-POWER MOVEMENT.'

GERI HALLIWELL
MUCH, 1997

'WHAT I PASSIONATELY FEEL IS THAT IT IS SO WRONG TO HAVE TO FIT INTO A ROLE OR A MOULD IN ORDER TO SUCCEED.'

GERI HALLIWELL

Vogue interview, January 1997

★

'IT FELT LIKE WE WERE ALL AT TH

CENTRE OF THE WORLD

FOR A MINUTE.'

GERI HALLIWELL
Guardian, 10 March 2018

'WE CREATED OURSELVES.'

MELANIE BROWN

The Late Show with Stephen Colbert, 18 January 2017

'AS FAR AS WE'RE CONCERNED,
ANY PRESS IS GOOD PRESS.'

VICTORIA BECKHAM

Rolling Stone magazine, 6 March 1997

'FROM THE BEGINNING OF OUR JOURNEY,
TWENTY-HOW-MANY YEARS AGO,
WE'VE ALWAYS PUT WHAT WE LOVE
AND BELIEVE FIRST.'

GERI HALLIWELL
The Jonathan Ross Show, 13 November 2018

'I DO HAVE A MASSIVE EGO — I ALWAYS HAVE
DONE, FAMOUS OR NOT.'

MELANIE BROWN
Guardian, 5 May 2017

'WE'RE REHEARSED I

OUT-OF-CONTROLNESS.'

MELANIE BROWN

Spice Girls — Wild! in Concert, 17 January 1998

'WE REALISED THAT WE WERE QUITE DIFFERENT PERSONALITIES, DIFFERENT TO EACH OTHER AND TO ALL THE FEMALE GROUPS IN THE PAST. WE ALSO REALISED THERE WAS A LOT OF STRENGTH IN THAT.'

MELANIE CHISHOLM
Guardian, 10th March 2018

'WE ALWAYS GO ON THE CONCEPT OF: WE'RE JUST NORMAL PEOPLE, AND THAT'S WHAT NORMAL PEOPLE ENJOY.'

EMMA BUNTON

Rolling Stone magazine, 10 July 2007

★

'FAME REALLY SIEVES OUT YOUR GOOD TRUE FRIENDS.'

MELANIE BROWN

The Oprah Winfrey Show, 1998

'FAME CAN BE TAKEN AWAY FROM YOU
AS QUICKLY AS IT'S GIVEN TO YOU.'

VICTORIA BECKHAM

MTV Europe Music Awards, 16 November 2000

'GO FOR IT AND DO EVERYTHING YOU WANT TO DO IN YOUR LIFE. LIFE'S TOO SHORT, YOU'VE GOT TO GO FOR IT.'

MELANIE CHISHOLM

Today Tonight interview, 1 December 1998

'I'VE WASTED SO MUCH TIME TRYING TO FINE-TUNE WHO I AM. NOW I TRY TO THINK, '"ACTUALLY, I'M ENOUGH. THIS IS GOING TO HAVE TO DO."'

GERI HALLIWELL

Guardian, 5 May 2017

'INSTEAD OF TRYING TO BE BETTER THAN SOMEONE ELSE, YOU HAVE TO TRY TO BETTER YOURSELF.'

MELANIE CHISHOLM

Vogue interview, January 1997

'IF THERE ARE RUMOURS ABOUT YOU, YOU MUST BE QUITE COOL FOR PEOPLE TO BE MAKING UP THINGS ABOUT YOU!'

EMMA BUNTON

Seventeen, 23 November 2007

♫

'YOU GET A PUNCH IN

THE FACE WHEN WE WALK IN.'

EMMA BUNTON

Lorraine, 12 November 2018

'MY FAMILY BROUGHT ME UP TO BE VERY
RESPECTFUL OF PEOPLE.'

EMMA BUNTON

Guardian, 18 November 2006

♬

'HEALTH AND FITNESS IS SO CURRENT,
I KIND OF FEEL LIKE, "WELL, I DID
TELL YOU ALL . . ."'

MELANIE CHISOLM
I News, 13 October 2016

♫

'I HAVE GOT MY OWN OPINION, I DO LIKE TO SAY EXACTLY WHAT I THINK AND I THINK PEOPLE AREN'T READY FOR THAT SOMETIMES. THEY'D RATHER HAVE SOMEONE QUIET AND SOMEONE WHO WILL AGREE TO EVERYTHING . . . FOR SOME PEOPLE THAT'S FRIGHTENING.'

MELANIE BROWN TO PRINCE

Paisley Park, 1998

♬

'IF YOU WANT TO FULFIL A DREAM,
YOU CAN GO OUT THERE AND DO IT.'

MELANIE BROWN

Today Tonight interview, 1 December 1998

♫

'I THINK THEY HAVE THIS IMPRESSION
THAT I'M THIS MISERABLE COW WHO
DOESN'T SMILE. BUT I'M ACTUALLY QUITE
THE OPPOSITE . . . I'M GOING TO TRY
AND SMILE MORE FOR AMERICA.'

VICTORIA BECKHAM
W magazine, 2007

'EXERCISE IS SUCH A GREAT THING FOR YOUR HEAD.'

MELANIE CHISHOLM

I News, 13 October 2016

'MY HEART IS ALWAYS

N BRITAIN'

GERI HALLIWELL
Spice Girls *GMTV* interview, 1997

'I WANT WORLD PEACE FOR CHRISTMAS.'

MELANIE BROWN

GMTV, December 1996

♫

'EVERY NOW AND AGAIN, I JUST GET UP
AND DO A BACK FLIP.'

MELANIE CHISHOLM

E! Now, 1997

'YOU NEVER KNOW WHAT'S AROUND
THE CORNER.'

GERI HALLIWELL
Manchester Evening News, 18 April 2010

'I GET INTO TROUBLE QUITE A LOT.'

GERI HALLIWELL

E! Now, 1997

MEN

'IT'S ABOUT SPREADING A
THE GIRLS…IT'S NO

WE DON'T NEED MEN

WE CONTRO

POSITIVE VIBE, KICKING IT FOR

ABOUT PICKING UP GUYS.

TO CONTROL OUR LIFE.

OUR LIVES ANYWAY.'

MELANIE BROWN

One Hour Of Girl Power, 1997

'GUYS HAVE ALWAYS BEEN TRICKY FOR ME.'

MELANIE CHISHOLM

Ruby Wax meets . . ., Series three, Episode 1, 1998

'BOYS WOULD COME ALONG, AND WE WERE SO CONNECTED – THE FIVE OF US GIRLS – BOYS WOULD HAVE TO CHECK THEM OUT, 'COS IF SOMEBODY CAME ALONG THAT MY FRIENDS DIDN'T LIKE, I DIDN'T LIKE THEM EITHER.'

EMMA BUNTON

Guardian, 18 November 2006

'YOU KNOW, I THINK

YOU'RE VERY SEXY.'

GERI HALLIWELL TO PRINCE CHARLES
Manchester Opera House, 1997

'COME AND HAVE A GO

IF YOU THINK
YOU'RE HARD ENOUGH.'

MELANIE CHISHOLM TO LIAM GALLAGHER
upon winning Best British Single at the Brit Awards, 1997

FRIENDSHIP

'WE ARE ALL SOULMATES AND LOVE EACH OTHER.'

MELANIE BROWN

The Big Breakfast interview, 6 March 1997

'I THINK THE WAY TO KEEP A FRIENDSHIP
IS TO RESPECT THAT EVERYBODY
IS DIFFERENT.'

EMMA BUNTON

Seventeen, 23 November 2007

❀

'I CAN'T IMAGINE

LIFE WITHOUT US.'

GERI HALLIWELL

Giving You Everything, 2007

'WE MIGHT NOT SEE EACH OTHER FOR MONTHS, BUT IF I NEED ONE OF THEM, THEY'LL BE THERE IN A MINUTE.'

EMMA BUNTON

Grazia, 7 July 2016

'WE DO SAY WHATEVER WE DO, WHEREVER WE GO, WE'RE GOING TO HAVE A LAUGH.'

VICTORIA BECKHAM
GMTV, December 1996

'THIS IS NOT MY JOB, THIS I
I WOULDN'T BE HER

MY LIFE AND MY GIRLS.
WITHOUT MY GIRLS.'

MELANIE BROWN
The Chris Evans Breakfast Show, 7 November 2018

'WE REALLY LOVED EACH

OTHER FOR REAL.'

GERI HALLIWELL
Giving you everything, 2007

'WE'RE SISTERS AT THE END OF THE DAY AND WHAT WE WENT THROUGH WAS QUITE AN AMAZING, BRILLIANT JOURNEY, SO WE'RE TOGETHER, WE'RE BACK TOGETHER.'

MELANIE BROWN

Loose Women, 23 July 2018

'FIVE GIRLS TOGETHER, WE LIKE TO
SPIN AROUND A POLE TOGETHER
EVERY NOW AND THEN.'

MELANIE BROWN

The Late Show with Stephen Colbert, 18 January 2017

'THE REAL TRUTH O

REALLY LOV

T IS, WE ACTUALLY

EACH OTHER.'

GERI HALLIWELL
The Dan Wootton Interview, 16 November 2018

'BECAUSE OF WHAT WE WENT THROUGH TOGETHER, THERE'S A BOND BETWEEN US THAT NO ONE ELSE WILL UNDERSTAND.'

EMMA BUNTON

Grazia, 7 July 2016

'I'M REALLY PROUD OF WHAT US FIVE GIRLS ACHIEVED OVER THE YEARS.'

MELANIE BROWN

The Late Late Show with James Corden, 14 September 2018

AT THE END OF THE DAY

E'RE JUST BEST MATES.'

MELANIE CHISHOLM
The Oprah Winfrey Show, 1998